A GLIMPSE AT LIFE

A Collection Of Poetry

by

Taylor Reese

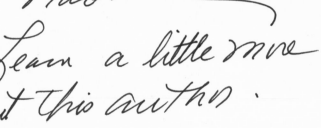

For Naomi —
Learn a little more
about this author.
Enjoy!

Taylor Reese

AAcorn Books
Micaville, North Carolina

Copyright © by Taylor Reese
2002

10 9 8 7 6 5 4 3 2 1

Cover Concept by Crispin Tovar
Cover Design by Morris Publishing
Page Design by Clothilde Vargas

Published by:

AAcorn Books
P. O. Box 647
Micaville, NC 28755-0647

ISBN: 0-9663666-7-0
Library of Congress Control Number: 2002103122

Printed in the United States of America
by
Morris Publishing
3212 East Highway 30, Kearney, NE 68847

This book is
dedicated to Margaret Painter,
a talented cousin,
whose poetry has been
an inspiration
for years

and

To all readers of poetry,
especially those who like
the eclectic.

Other books by Taylor Reese:

HUMOR IS WHERE YOU FIND IT
Look No Further
HUMOR AND A LITTLE BIT MORE
and
FROM HERE TO THERE
A Boy's Tale

Other books, written with co-author Jack R. Pyle:

RAISING WITH THE MOON
The Complete Guide to Gardening
and Living
by the Signs of the Moon

and

YOU AND THE MAN IN THE MOON
The Complete Guide to Using the Almanac

CONTENTS

Nature

The Teacher	1	Novembertime	16
Justification	2	Leaves	16
A Lesson	3	The Porch Is Empty	17
On Balance	4	I Wait	18
Cicadas	5	Twin Trees	20
Camouflage	5	Life	21
Bouquet	5	On People	21
Trees	6	The North Carolina	
"Spring"	6	Symphony	22
In Peaceful Search	6	Seasons	22
Charlotte		Verity	23
To New Orleans	7	Old Age	23
The Honey Bee	7	The Thinning Forest	24
The Circle Fades	8	Tested	25
Carolina Cycling	9	The Bee	25
Waves	9	Proof	26
Our Lady,		Directionals	26
The Dandelion	10	Flat	26
His Energy	10	The Clouds	
The Darkness of Nature	11	and Sun	27
Tomorrow	11	Celo Nob	27
Those Flying	12	Timely Attention	28
The Foggy Sign	12	Time	28
An Example	13	Out of Sync	29
A Need	14	The Precarious Web	29
Hope	14	Openers	30
Listen	14	Painting	32
"Aged Incisor"	15	Gardening	32
Independence	15	Human Nature	33
Positive	16	Life's Journey	34

Encouragement

Sunday	37	We Aged Do Repeat	54
Knowledge		Years	54
Is Worthy	38	Underjudged	55
Meltings	38	Too Late	55
Independence	38	If	55
Inevitable	39	In Need	56
Needed Dress	39	The Lover's Porch	56
Reincarnation	40	Now	56
Share	40	Plumage Affection	56
The Plan	40	Sixty-Five	57
Do It Now	41	Status Quo	57
Your Way	41	Youth/Age	58
WeCare	42	Brainless	58
Solution	43	Brainless Two	58
Comfort	43	The Difference	59
People Inhabit the Earth	44	Welfare	59
Correction Needed	44	"Delight"	60
Incomplete Evidence	45	Fact	60
A Talk With Him	46	Departure/Arrivals	60
S I N	47	Despite	61
Still More	48	Is There	61
The Stars Can Help	48	The Aerial Way	61
Onward	49	She, Too	62
He Knows	50	Penchant	62
Acceptance	51	Human Law	62
		Comparison	63

Humor

		Infactual	63
		Meant To Be	63
Good/Bad	53	More Welfare	64
A Sign to Show	53	Considerate	64
Weighty Comment	53	Tissue	65
Problem	54	Less Critical	65

Compensation	66	Gracious Me!	80
Harmony	66	The Aging Gent	81
Observation	67	Beauty	81
Overweight	67	Differences	81
Ramblings	67	Gambling	82
Zodiacally Speaking	68	Seventy-Nine	82
They Say	69	Hair	82
Jagged	69	Working Together	83
The Heads	69	Reminder	83
Addiction	70	Replacement	84
Originality	71	Oh, Yes	85
Misplaced Love	71	Life's Unsavory Recipe	85
Congregate	72	Mental Patchwork	
Excuse	72	In A Relationship	85
Lacking	72		
Future	72		
Flout	73	**Miscellany**	
Jottings	73		
Synthetic Stones	73	Our Flag	87
Slab/Tab	74	Quo Vadis	88
Because	74	The Cemetery Tree	89
You're Right	75	Furrow	90
A Hope	76	No Longer The Place	90
Look First	76	Foreign Policy	91
For All To See	76	In Pursuit Of What?	91
On This Plane	77	Ode to Momus	92
Over Seventy	77	Love's Collection	93
Waste	77	Sickness	94
Mr. Piggy (In Flight)	78	Aid	94
A Fact	78	Ditto	94
Susie, The Sow	79	Outlook	95
The Recycling Center	79	Emotional Antonyms	95

The Aphrodisiac	95	AGING IS:	112
Suspension	96	Opportunity	112
Dim Hope	96	The Final	113
If Given	97	My Trips	114
Quandary	97	Passing	114
Opinion	97	ThePorch	114
Await	98	The Doctor's	
Attitude	98	Receptionist	115
The Fact	99	The Others	115
Companion	99	Words	116
Democracy	99	Utopian Dream	116
Gauging	100	Unwarranted Treatment	116
Time	100	Crossroads	117
In Charge	100	A Guidepost	117
Instincts	101	Why?	118
Mankind	101	A Deed In Defeat	118
Horizons	102	Life's Facade	118
Metamorphosis	103	Misjudging	118
It Is Within	103	Room 620	119
Myself	104	More Care	119
Needs	104	The Way	119
Treasures	104	The Troubled World	120
The Homeless One	105	Mortal	120
Counsel	106	Lonesome At	
Cliffhanging	106	The Airport	121
Our Brethren	107	Friends	122
Surprises	108	Gutter Inlet	122
Sightless Observation	108	Happiness	123
Dosage	109	J U S T I C E	124
The SoreMakers	109	The Wealthy At The Inn	126
From Obscurity		Entwined	126
To Oblivion	110	Hate	126
Some of the Past	110	Life - A Three Act Play	127
The Stairs	111	Clover	128

A Woman's Dream   128
Hopeful   128
Hollow Legacy   129
Time Marches On   130
An Opinion   130
Without Enrichment   131
"A Friend"   131
A Sea   132
In Spite Of   132
His Brother's Funeral   133
In School Today   133
Randy   134
An Honest
    Opportunity   135
TORO DE LIDIA   136

NATURE

Man's Greatest Asset

The Teacher

Despite man's desperate attempt
    to rule the Universe,
Mother Nature has its way of
    putting him in his place
(sometimes harshly, sometimes gently),
Because she knows moderation and balance
    are the key.
She questions not his silly goals,
Nor passes judgment on acts of crime,
But arrives upon the scene in ways
    he can't reject,
And then sits back and waits
    to see if he will learn.

Justification

It was a moment of reverie

In the morning hours

Before the sun devoured

The mystery of dawn.

All life lay quiet

At the feet of time,

Waiting for movement

Throughout the earthly plane—

A signal that all creatures

Have a purpose and a natural right

To be a part of His creation.

A Lesson

Happy Birds

singing their tunes

waken us each day

and know not what

we seek in life,

nor really care.

Each is content

to build its home

raise its young

train them well

release them

and begin the cycle again

(so simple, so clear, so desired),

but man has yet to learn

from Nature's master plan.

On Balance

Some love the clouds
　　　that quietly roam the skies,
And trees that bow to Nature's whim,
But I prefer both man and beast
　　　because of their strange union.

They seem so contrastingly alike:
　　　One fights to survive,
　　　The other survives to fight.

Each thinks of self:
　　　One to live with man,
　　　The other to kill him off.

Both are filled with aim:
　　　One to fill a need,
　　　The other to conquer more.

Neither is here for long:
　　　One to balance Nature,
　　　The other to change its course.

Likely, neither will win:
　　　One because he's overpowered,
　　　The other because he overpowers.

Cicadas

Cicadas' abdominal membranes vibrate
In monotonous song night in, night out.
They are really stringing us along—
Winter, no doubt.

Camouflage

Each snowflake falls gently down
And brings a message for us that's clear.
It is to smile and hide the frown
That love can bring while it is near.

Bouquet

Compliments are but flowers
    in the vase of life,
Sometimes moved
    and strewn about.
And yet they still remain
    the thing we need the most
To keep the lifeline
    from a drought.

The
trees I
like within my
yard need not be so
tall and straight as long
as they provide the shade
that hides the sun and help to
in
su
late.

"Spring"

Acres of words
     planted just right
Bring forth growth
     that's beautiful and bright.

In Peaceful Search

Clouds above
Have spaced themselves
In patterned beauty—white and free.
They roam without a care
Because they know that man
In all his expertise
Cannot alter their course
As they search the skies
In valiant effort to help
Him coexist.

Charlotte To New Orleans

The clouds we glide above reach far,

    far toward the horizon.

But I see beyond

    a blue that never ends,

    a light and easy blue.

It is so clear, so crisp, so comforting,

    I know it reaches forever—

    and dares to treat us all alike.

The Honey Bee

If all mankind
Were like the honeybee—
No fuss, just work—
What a world to see.

The Circle Fades

Why has winter come
    so soon
And dropped the blooms of summer?
They were my friends,
    and family, too,
Who gave me hope,
    and joy and love.
They asked not
    whence I came,
    nor when I planned to go.
It was enough
    that each be each,
But now
    that can no longer be,
    because
God has His plan—
    and man knows not why;
Some accept it,
    others cry.

Carolina Cycling

Summer has passed
    and Fall is ebbing.
The leaves sprinkle earthward,
      moved only by wind or man.
Finally, Nature wins
    and keeps them for its own,
Knowing winter is close behind
    to play its role
Before Spring again
    takes the lead,
And adds its youthful thrust
    to help repeat the cycle,
Thus showing man
    life really is eternal.

Waves

The waves out there are blue and brisk.
They rush upon the shores.
Each seems to have an asterisk
That asks for more encores.

9

Our Lady, The Dandelion

Our Dandelion is a spunky flower,
Popping up each day, she does not cower.
There is no doubt she is not regional,
Though everyone knows she is quite seasonal.

Bursting forth at sunrise in early Spring,
Splashing color, a beautiful thing.
Before the gray globe comes the pretty sets
And always dozens of little florets.

She never fails to be obedient
At sunset's closing when the day is spent,
And gives us each a sign, a prayerful hope
For all in the world who need to cope.

Now don't forget, she is quite friendly,
And asks that she not be pampered so keenly,
But when you learn her name you may well dally,
It is: *ta-rax-a-cum of-fi-ci-nal-e.*

His Energy

We harness all the energy we can
And draw on many sources, too.
Occasionally He says, "You overran,
So stop the course you now pursue."

You'd think we'd learned our lesson well
So there'd be no need to cower.
Our only hope: Do not rebel
Against the use of "soul-ar" power.

10

The Darkness of Nature

The stars are not dancing tonight
And the Moon is down under.
The owl perches, scanning,
In search of a meal.
Innocently, the mouse romps
Amid a field of cut wheat.
Death will soon be his brother—
His body enriching another.
The soul will move on,
Wherever souls go.
Nature's need fulfilled.

Tomorrow

My window shows a mountaintop
In front of all the heavy clouds.
It needs no special type of prop
Despite the evil it enshrouds.

Tomorrow it will still be there—
The clouds removed, replaced by sun.
A sign of blue and all that's fair,
The chance to say it has begun.

A life that's new, one made from hope
And filled with time for each of us
To scan our lives that seem so taupe
And leaves us each sans stimulus.

Those Flying

Birds are the creatures made by God
Though often neglected by man.
They are the ones that afford joy,
And we should help them all we can.

I've watched them as they pick and scratch
Through low thickets far and near,
And without fail they seem to know
They have no cause to fear.

Though their wild instinct is to be alert
I know they think man is a friend,
One with whom they can communicate
And feel no reason to offend.

The Foggy Sign

Soft gray settles
Between the mountaintops
Thin layers skim the peaks
Stillness reigns for a moment
As green grass gives hope
While tall conifers offer life
Showing Nature at its best,
Telling mankind it must adhere—
Or lose and suffer.

An Example (In Flight)

Scattered clouds
>float aimlessly
>below,
Yet above man's structures,
>asking only
>that they be permitted
>to roam undisturbed
>as we glide through the air
To points of:
>frustration
>fanaticism
>peace
>finalization.

A Need

A calmness holds the scene outside:
No sun, no wind, just floating clouds
That gently stroke the mountain's pride
To warn us each of closer vows.

Hope

Azure blue skies above
Soft white clouds below
Are trying to show man
Peace is possible
If each remains
Within his realm.

Listen!

If we listen carefully
Mother Nature tells us much.
She teaches us the value
Of staying close in touch.

"Aged Incisor"

Though old and drawn with lines of age,
She stood erect and faced the man.
The look was not that of a sage,
Nor one that lived a life of plan.

It was instead a mark of life
You see among some kindly folk:
Despair and lots of daily strife,
Along with signs of being broke.

Her heart was big, her smile sincere.
The voice was weak, the hair unkempt.
It was her tooth that made me fear
There was a chance for some contempt.

But when she smiled and bowed her head,
And turned it to the side a bit,
I knew she was ashamed instead
To show the tooth and then admit

It was the only one she had
Within her mouth to chew and eat,
And not because it was a fad,
But simply Nature's way to cheat.

Independence

Try not to lose your faith in man
Across the expanse we call the earth;
Instead, begin the magic plan
And look to Him for rebirth.

Positive

As the outer fades
        the inner grows
A sign of acceptance —
        though reluctantly —
That life is positive.

Novembertime

As Fall
Begins to fade
It tells us all for sure
That winter's close behind
With all its lure.

Leaves

As they are raked both to and fro

The leaves care not in the least

As long as they are used again

As mulch to bring the Springtime feast.

The Porch is Empty

The porch is empty
Save a few chairs
And me in one.

I gaze across the road
Above the green trees.
A buzzard glides by,

And I raise my eyes still higher
To see a panorama
Unlike any other.

For way out there
Lies beauty to behold
The green majestic mountains.

They are so calm,
So quiet, so friendly
In their graceful form.

One knows, without further search,
That peace lies all around,
If only one stops to *live*.

I Wait

It is early yet
By standards of some,
And Asheville is moist, damp and foggy
As I sit in my car in the allotted space.

I sit patiently, silently and alone
Awaiting one and only one,
And while this wait occurs
I hear the city coming alive.

On streets around and below,
What once was inactivity,
Quelled by early dawn,
Is now changing to a hum, a roar, a bustle.

It smacks of people enroute
To work, to assignments, to appointments,
Or just somewhere—
Maybe the library, the pool hall or lounge.

As this human mass moves to and fro
It carries with it the stench of city crowds.
Unafraid, a squirrel runs down a nearby tree—
A breath of hope for all mankind.

But borne along with this unavoidable stench
There is an air of confidence,
Industriousness and aim.
And it is through this caring attitude,

This apparent desire for common goal,
A goal of existence, better and longer,
That this city, Asheville,
Will be a haven for thousands more in times to come.

It will be a city of enlightenment
For those seeking better climes,
Better health, better times,
And as it stands high among the mountains

It will offer to all who enter its gates,
The best, the most of kindness in living.
Asheville, the city of charm and warmth,
Is now awake, humming and bustling with people,

People who like it,
People who will grow as it grows.
Long may it serve as a mecca for all —
Asheville, the City Bountiful.

Twin Trees

Nearly a hundred years ago
    Nature began another of its many
    unparalleled feats when they
    sprung forth, anxious to contribute,
    standing tall in the parking lot of the park.

They grew, became closer to one another until they
    finally entwined,
    causing their lives to change
    because they were now one,
    and would grow and each support the other.

They grew in graceful form,
    a slight curvature outward
    until they became bigger,
    and today they are a tower of stability,
    a statue of beauty admired by many —

Symbols of yesterday's chance
    and today's hope and tomorrow's opportunity
    to all who want to live
    with Nature's constant attempt
    to show mankind we are one, and for a reason.

Life

Life is like a budding leaf
    opening with tenderness.
And when reaching maturity
    unique beauty awaits
    Nature's call
    to relinquish its fullness,
Where its last performance is in color
    before the final act completes
    the cycle intended, and lets it fall,
Only to be left—at least for a while—
Before metamorphosis, regeneration
    and rebirth.

On People

New friendships are like a breath of Spring,
Old ones like the predictiveness of Fall.
Lost friendships are the dismal dead of winter,
And new acquaintenances a summer treat.

The North Carolina Symphony
(In Outdoor Concert)

The sun inched downward
Lightly touched the mountaintops
Rimmed them each with gold
Balanced there for just a while
Then slid down the other side
And left for us an emerald isle.
The strings, the brass, percussions and winds
Filled our hearts and ears
Brought us to our rested feet
Because we were so pleased
Our hunger, yes, appeased.

Seasons

Youth - a bed of Spring flowers

Maturity - a field of summer growth

Midlife - Fall's harvest season

Old Age - Winter's hidden larder

Verity

Time metastasizes youth,
Crystallizes maturity,
And penalizes old age.
There is no cure,
No deterrent,
No lesser price to pay.

Old Age

With its unyielding influence,

Time wrinkled her face,

Curved her body,

Altered her mind,

Showing each of us

Nothing remains the same,

Except time

With it unyielding influence.

The Thinning Forest

Once prolific—
    all kinds and ages—
Now young growth abounds
    offering mingling pleasures
    a place to share secrets
    a haven when in need of solace
And through the years Nature
    in its discerning wisdom
    decreed that some live on and on
    while others fell
    to the whims of merciless time
    and the Master's will
Until today it is sparse beyond belief
    as I gaze around
    and feel so akin
    yet know that "tomorrow"
    I, too, will contribute
    to the thinning forest
    I call "family."

Tested

Jagged rocks, aged stones,
Sands afoot and earth beneath
Brave Nature's role,
Offer all a better foundation,
For they, more than we,
Know full well the Master Plan:
Birth, survival, death,
A cycle never broken...for long.

The Bee

The bee
A tiny thing
Smoothly flies his way
Over the hills and over the dells
To see that man is fed with sweet
Each day.

Proof

I've delved into facts of all mankind
That claim to make me click,
And yet I cannot seem to find one truth,
Not one that makes it stick.

Directionals

Life is just a compass
Pointing in different directions
At different times
Depending on circumstances.

Flat

I know the world is round,
The wheels in charge said so,
But had He made it flat
A lot more things would grow.

The Clouds and Sun

Each day unfolds with clouds and sun
And asks that I choose
The one that offers me the fun
Lest I be one to lose.
And would you think that I'm aware
Of both, and what they bring,
As each of them so rightly share
The best of everything?

Celo Nob

The mountain rises above all men
Holds its stance with no regret
For it knows where it stands
And offers help to those who fail
Whose heads hang low
And minds bow lower.

It asks that they look upward
Toward its peak
Because there lies beneath its crest
A hope, a guide, a chance
To glimpse its message
A message to go onward...

With Purpose, With Strength, With Joy.

Timely Attention

Outside we mingle
    with the man on the street
    the farmer in the field
    a tiny child at play.
At home we interact
    with family
    enjoy each one of them
    throughout the fleeting day.
But it is with the inner self
    we always need to deal
    (so wisely, so firmly)
    Lest much could pass away
And little we'll have done
    ere ends our allotted term.

Time

Time is the greatest thing we have
For it allows us freedom to be.

Out of Sync

If one begins to think of man
As one who helps the Universe,
We have to then admit the plan
Has left us each with quite a curse.

A curse so huge and deeply veined
It's doubtful now in our lifetime
We'll see relief for each so pained,
And all because there is no natural rhyme.

The Precarious Web

Life is a spider's web
Hanging precariously in the wind,
Always subject
To the whims of chance.

While beauty it may hold,
It is only a limited time
Before Nature comes in
And asks the spinner to begin again.

Openers

My world was small and close and friendly.
The trees offered beauty, shade and solace.
The animals were my friends,
And the masses were humane.

But then I grew;
My eyes were open wide,
And the world kept on—
It always will.

Until today.
The forests are now sparse,
The animals are too scarce
And afraid to be my friends.

People have lost their kindly need to need,
Replaced it with greed and power.
And man's use of time renders our world a
Difficult place in which to live.

Will we become entombed
In our own doings,
And lie in state for those who come after
To view and pay "respects"?

Or will they speak in anger
At what we have done?
Only time and its undaunted meanderings
(Abused by man) will give the answer.

Others who come later
Will heap blame or praise,
As they, too, render judgment
Through their jaundiced eyes.

Man is not helpless;
He just does not care.
He feels an urge to act, and does,
Whether for good or bad.

But he renders unto himself and others
That which is deserved,
And then is dissatisfied,
Never stopping to realize...
it is his own undoing.

Painting

Painting is the act by some
Of placing on canvas—
Be it of whatever medium—
That which they see or sense or feel.

Both from within
Or from without
The result, of course,
Is colored by pride and prejudice,

As well as warmth
And life's experiences.
It gives an aura of
Authenticity beyond belief,

For these sensitive and talented creatures—
Too few and far between—
Are more highly tuned into the Universe
Than we who merely breathe and view.

Gardening

All things are equal
Given time to grow
But we must be aware
Much depends
On how we sow.

Human Nature

Man's differences remain the same;

It is the degree of tolerance

That alters the game.

Life's Journey

It begins so insignificantly,
      so innocently,
Then growth becomes a habit
      until we reach
Our youthful prime.

Choices then appear:
      some good, some bad,
      some in between.

Knocks we take,
      praise we like,
Friends we make,
      enemies we disdain.
(In either case, at our command.)

We spiral upward
      or downward,
(depending on the goal and perseverance).

And then resign ourselves
      (by choice or force)
To slacken our pace,
      let time move on
As we slow down,

Until, finally,
       we stand still,
       as helpless as at birth.

The moment nears
       when it is over
And we no longer seek
       but ask that He allow us
       to leave

And return again
       into the unknown
       to pause there in peace,

In whole,
       until He
       sees fit
       to use us again.

ENCOURAGEMENT

From Many Sources

Sunday

Pews of sin
      crowd the calling house,
      tinged with godliness.
Outside
      critters of time,
      enmeshed with reality,
      beg their daily existence,
      and offer unto the world
      a truthfulness far surpassing
      the human lemmings
      who flock the sanctioned space,
      hoping to be among those chosen
      by a higher power.
In time, each will be rewarded:
      by Him, by mankind, or by self.

Knowledge Is Worthy

The years we live upon this land
Are set by God at time of birth.
We know there is no real demand
Except to spread our inner worth.

Meltings

God gave us many people
with lots of little minds,
And most, alas, are here to stay
because it takes all kinds.

Independence

Try not to lose your faith in man
Across the expanse we call this earth;
Instead, begin the magic plan
And look to Him for that new birth.

Inevitable

No need to weep when those so near
Begin their final trip afar
Because the Master Overseer
Will make worthwhile the au revoir.

Just as He chooses times for birth,
And tries His best to keep us straight,
He lets us each remain on Earth —
Assigned allotted times by fate.

Needed Dress

Look not to others for comfort;

Too often they are ill-clothed.

Better to seek a robe

Woven from inner strength.

Reincarnation

All things in life that come to man
Are good or bad or in between,
And each of them, I'm sure, began
Before he came upon the scene.

Share

Kindness ranks high with some,
    low with others.
It is a gift for all to hoist
    throughout the world.

The Plan

They say Almighty God
Is big and strong and knows us all.
I can't this disregard,
But, why do so many fall?

It seems to me the Plan
Would be a fairer one indeed
If He assigned each man
A job to live and work by God's own Creed.

Do It Now

One acts as if the thing to do
To keep the soul alive and well
Is eat and sleep but not review
Before we say our last farewell.

I think if all who want to learn
The way to keep the soul in tune
Would just begin to try to earn
A walk with Him 'twould help—and soon.

Your Way

It doesn't matter whether you live
        to be old,
Or whether you die young—
        And that is a relative thing—
What does matter is the attitude and
        actions while here.

If they are positive and constructive,
        with consideration for others,
You will have made the necessary contribution
        to the overall picture.
That's all God asks;
        never mind what man says.

WeCare
(Nursing Home)

Years trampled her body,
Impoverished her mind,
Leaving only bits of yesterday.

Technology stepped in,
Offered perpetual care,
Family and friends were there.

She was not.

Years trampled her body,
Impoverished her mind,
Leaving only bits of yesterday.

Now WeCare can do no more,
Nor family, nor friends.
Only God.

Solution

Just as the growing child
Is overwhelmed at the complexities
    of life,
So, apparently are many world leaders today.
The solution is so simple,
If all would follow:
"Do unto others
    as you would have them do unto you."

Comfort

We have to learn our lessons well
If in His house we are to dwell.
And once we've passed that simple test,
A place is made for peaceful rest.

People Inhabit the Earth

People inhabit the Earth,
    for what, they do not know.
Some say it's God's plan,
    others do not say.
They inhabit the Earth
    awaiting tomorrows,
Tomorrows that may not come,
    but they still inhabit the Earth.

Correction Needed

If God had known when He began

To fill this world with man and beast

How far afield His plan would go,

He would, I'm sure, have tried at least

To temper down the man aspect,

And build up the beast instead.

Because they show some real respect

Before they're each among the dead.

Incomplete Evidence

I read the sign outside the church of God:
"I am so glad He set me free."
Perplexed by those inside who got the nod
Because they simply paid their fee.

I spoke with Him in privacy,
And asked if He would give a clue
About the ones who felt such legacy
Was theirs indeed a rightful due.

His voice fell gently on my ears,
Without attempt to judge my ken.
He asked that I go kindly on the dears
Because they were my fellowmen.

Some time went by with that inside my craw.
Convinced the proof was lacking still,
I searched to try and find the irksome flaw
Or learn the Master's precious will.

The Man upstairs again did speak
To let me hear a further clue:
"Forgive the ones who strive to feign and sneak
Because they know not what they do."

A Talk With Him

I had a talk with Him above
To learn His thoughts of me.
And when it came to push and shove
I was His legacy.

But then the things I thought were great
He marked as *ordinaire,*
And left me in a qualmish state:
"Thy soul," He said, "repair."

I let Him know I felt a blank
About the things He sought.
He told me how to walk the plank
To do the things I ought.

His list was long and quite exact,
And left no room for doubt.
I was to let no one detract
His charge to be devout.

SIN

In the eyes of some
Sin is an act by man
Judged wrong
By another.

And who, I boldly ask—
At least among we mortals here—
Can freely sit in judgment
Of our fellowman?

Sin to me
May be honor to you.
Pleasure for me
May be sin for you.

I suspect our fairest stance would be
To sit in judgment,
Oh, yes,
But only of thyself.

And if we must be judged,
Let not it be by others,
But leave it to the conscience within
And the Judge above.

Still More

We've reached the peak
    and only look down.
How great it would be
    atop it all,
    to look upward, yes,
Toward yet a higher goal.

The Stars Can Help

Tonight the sky is filled with stars
And each is shining bright and clear.
Not one is filled with great memoirs
That tell us all of yesteryear.

They send instead a hope indeed
For all the world to see and grasp,
That each upon this earth in need
Can help if hands are in a clasp.

Onward

People, like cars,
Are not made to last,
And some have scars
From an awful past.

Though many are pleased
With the way they live,
Others appeased
Or contributive.

We know each one
Is essential here. . .
The Master's plan
For the hemisphere.

He Knows

Our Lord above does surely know
The ones who serve Him well.
He also sees the things below
And those that lean toward Hell.

The time will come for Him to judge
The good we've done for all,
And check the ones who tried to fudge,
Then said, "I don't recall."

And when He makes His rightful choice,
Surprised He'll be to find
The ones who had the loudest voice
Were not the ones that He designed.

Acceptance

The question now is what to do

    About the stage I'm passing through.

It's called "old age" by some who know

    And have the proof they seem to show.

We have advice from experts near

    That does not make it disappear,

But does somehow make me think

    There is, I'm sure, some interlink

Between the years we spend on earth

    And what we do that brings us worth:

In health, in friends, in family, too,

    Before we reach our rendezvous.

HUMOR

Here, There and About

Good/Bad

Each heart is filled with lots of good
And just a bit of bad.
Oh what a shame dear Robin Hood
Could not have been my dad.

A Sign To Show

The age
Of each of us
Is but a sign to show
That time and place and things
We do outgrow.

Weighty Comment

I'm of the opinion
The reason people stand out
Is not from deed and thought
But because of appetite.

Problem

The only problem young people have
    is *youth;*
And, unfortunately, too often years
    do not cure it.

We Aged Do Repeat

The God above did bless us all
When He bestowed upon the old
The right for those who don't recall
To hear the tales again retold.

Years

I don't mind old age,
Nor the many of my own years,
But why all the rage
About their yesteryears?

Underjudged

We're told that time does help to heal
The ills incurred by broken hearts.
But why does one just not reveal
They lack too much in plain old smarts?

Too Late

Along the way my mother said,
"My son, if you don't watch the squint
"The time will come that you will dread
"The lines around those eyes that glint."

A picture sure of facial age,
And all because I had to squint.
It made me look unlike a sage
And caused the girls to give no hint.

So then I stood and saw myself
As others viewed me in the face
'Twas then I knew I was no elf,
And yet too late to youth embrace.

If

If faces were wallpaper,
Most people with good taste
Would paint, not paper.

In Need

If accomplishment were measured by thinking,
    some would be rich and others poor;
Yet both would still be lacking
    and need a whole lot more.

The Lover's Porch

My porch is large
And can seat them all
But now I'm old
And it is Fall.

Now

In our fast world today

Living to a ripe old age

Is anywhere beyond the moment.

Plumage Affection

If Santa Claus had not chosen Prancer
He would have had no problem with Dancer,
But when he hitched them both together
They became like "birds of a feather."

Sixty-Five

Nothing arrives faster
    nor is less welcomed
        than age.

Its only rewards:
    Social Security, Medicare
        and a convenient memory loss.

Status Quo

If you fail
    where others succeed,
    just let it be.
There is
    a lack
    of pure equality.

Youth/Age

How marvelous
    to see youth in age.
Now if we could only see
    age in youth.

Brainless

God gave us each a brain
And expects us to use it.
You can only gain
Or maybe lose it.

Brainless Two

God gave me a brain

And said, "Use it."

I thought he said "pain,"

So refused it.

The Difference

If man were asked to choose
      between fine food and lovely girls,
No doubt they'd all become quite stout.

* * *

If women were asked to choose
      between fine food and handsome men,
No doubt they'd all become quite thin.

Welfare

God chose the ones He thought were right

To lend a hand and help

But did not contemplate a blight

Of "lazies" born to yelp.

"Delight"

The rooster sits upon his roost,
Awaits the hen's invite.
He needs no real or helping boost,
Because her name's "Delight."

Fact

I only saw my face,
And glimpsed the body space.
'Twas then I really knew
It's time you can't erase.

Departures/Arrivals

Nothing is more definite
Than printed airline schedules,
And nothing more indefinite
Than adherence to those schedules.

Despite

If age treated us all alike
And left the rest to us
Somewhere down the human pike
There'd still be room to fuss.

Is There?

Is there within this world
Someone who's meant to be
That special sexy girl
Who wants to be with me?

I've searched both far and wide
To find a soul like that,
But those I've known have lied
Or else been Democrat.

The Aerial Way

Airplanes aren't on time,
But babies crying
And hyenna laughs
Are a guarantee
If one flies with regularity.

She, Too

Why have you filed the things I've said
O'er all the years gone by?
Do not you know I'm, yes, inbred
Which makes us now a tie.

Penchant

Tell me, oh great and wondrous one,
Why life today brings such dismay?
Is it because of what I've done
Or just because you like to bray?

Human Law

Sex is my native tongue,
Love my second language;
Marriage is foreign soil,
And divorce alien space.

Comparison

If all the things that men now want
Were put within their reach,
I think they'd still go out and flaunt
Their bodies on the beach.

Now ladies have the right to flirt
And do it all the time,
But mostly men are there alert
To show they're in their prime.

Infactual

Mirror, mirror on the wall

Are you really the most cracked of all?

If that is indeed the case,

Then I have excuse for this old face.

Meant To Be

All things in life are meant to be,

So say the ones who claim to know,

But don't you think the rest of us

Deserve a chance to disagree?

More Welfare

If welfare seems
    an obsession to me,
It is because it's anything
    but free.
Such cost, if borne
    by thee,
I would not mind,
    but when I pay,
I wish another kind.

Considerate

She chose to speak her mind,
Then closed the lips at once,
Because it was not kind
To say the words about the dunce.

Tissue

Here I hang
Completely ignored,
At your disposal
All the time.
I never complain
Of over usage.
I do my best
To satisfy,
And yet
You seldom think of me
Except in case
Of necessity.

Less Critical

One has to overlook the faults
Of those he calls his friends
And try to lessen all the "oughts"
Or else become has-beens.

Compensation?

Death has its benefits
And life its disadvantages,
But both are counterfeits
That keep us simple hostages.

Harmony

There is no need to beat your gums
In hopes she'll see the light.
She'll always want more freebie plums;
She thinks it is her right.

* * *

Life is meaningless without good aim,
And what a pity that is.
Think of the price paid for the game
Just thinking he's quite the whiz.

Observation

I watched
As he came on board.
And while I cannot quarrel with God
And His attempt with man,
When He made the face
He was no artisan.

Overweight

It is too sad our life on earth
Is not judged by solely girth.
Be that the case, I am quire sure
We'd all be rich, and, yes, secure.

Ramblings

Some of my hair has gone A W O L,
        and that that hasn't is threatening to.

Think of nagging as negotiation by only one party.

Zodiacally Speaking

Gregory Gregarious
    was born Aquarius
And found Aries
    was quite the breeze
But dropped dear Taurus
    the money walrus
And sought quick Gemini
    whose wit was dry

Though next was Cancer
    certainly no prancer
Then looked to Leo
    who was quite the hero
But ole Virgo
    had nothing to show
So he balanced with Libra
    whose name was Hybra

And then fast Scorpio
    yanked on his yo-yo
Of course, Sagittarius
    just blurted, "Praise us"
And poor Capricorn
    was heaped with scorn
But, alas, there was Pisces
    Ill with Zodiac Disease.

Poor Gregory...

They Say

They say all work, no play
    will make the boy quite dull.
It does, though, help defray
    to keep the lazy cull.

Jagged

Words of Praise
Fall easily from her lips
But somehow
Before they reach my ears
They turn to pebbles
And jagged ones at that.

The Heads

The heads I see aboard this plane
Are like a field of spotted grain:
The brown, the red, the black, the gray,
And blue that's used the garish way.

But none assert that special right
Like some who wear the snowy white,
Nor those who've passed the thinning line
And send a beam via Nature's shine.

Addiction

When we hear "addiction" today
We think of alcohol and drugs.
But I suffer not from either
Of those dreadful types.

They're foreign to my soul,
Alien to my body.
Though "addiction"
I have not escaped.

You see, it's simple,
And yet a pity, too,
That mine rests with just
A bit too much good stuff.

Good, they say, in many ways,
But I know its abuse
Brings forth problems.
So what am I to do?

Oh, suffer through
This crippling siege,
And hope some day to find
IceCreamaholics Anonymous.

Originality

Her name, they say, was Maudi,
Though some, I'm told, yelled "Sadie."
And while a wee bit bawdy,
She was indeed a lady.

When asked, she'd do a favor,
Regardless of the type;
Expected you to savor
In hopes there'd be no gripe.

Misplaced Love

He shot the arrow without aim
And then began to quickly claim
The cause for such a tragic miss
Was due to her and blindful bliss.

She quickly pushed aside the blame
And asked her name he not defame,
"Because," she said, "do not forget,
It's man that's beast, a lowly pet."

Congregate

Mary and Joseph were in the stable
Not because they were unable,
But what better place to congregate
Then spread a fantastic fable.

Excuse

She says her heart is torn
From years of much abuse
And knows he is not worn
Just uses that excuse.

Lacking

No one knows the trouble I've seen,
Nor do they really care.
It's not that I'm fat or lean,
It's less and less of hair.

Future

I was not born yesterday
And probably won't die tomorrow.
I cannot help my past,
But look forward to the future
Without a bit of horror.

Flout

There's nothing wrong with inlaws.
As long as they are out,
But when you start to see the flaws,
The "in" could become the "out."

Jottings

I can write you numerous things
Because I am many people
And much without the strings
Attached to church and steeple.

Synthetic Stones

I read and hear that greats live on and on,
And simply can't refute the fact,
But some are just plain zircons
Wrapped in glitter to attract.

Slab/Tab

Rest my body on the slab;
Take your pencil, check the tab.
If I've indeed made the grade,
Then let me go without a trade.

Because, you see, our life on earth
Is not meant to be all mirth,
But if we seek to just comply,
There's very little left to try.

And so with that in mind,
Don't reach out and try to find
Other traits or deeds that count,
Cause I'm ready for the mount.

And when I'm on up high above
Think not of peace and snow white dove;
Think, instead, of me,
And please, my friend, just let it be.

Because

We know that man lives not alone
By bread and wine and scone.
He does, in fact, subsist because
He fails to scratch the marriage clause.

74

"You're Right"

You're right, they aren't Gucci;
They're Sears.
Oh, the suit?
What do you think?
No, not K-Mart.
Want to try for Wal-Mart?

Oh, the tie?
Why? Don't you like it?
It is Pierre Cardin. Really.
Although from the marked-down table.

So, by what do you judge a man?

If it's personality, I am quite wealthy.
In looks I am comfortably situated.
Health, better than many.
Financial, secure.

A Hope

I came in broke,
And I spent every cent—
Earned or lent—
And I went out broke.

Look First

No one will argue with the fact
Some people are vague and quite abstract,
But what will always bring about a row
Is if you dare to disallow
Their right to be an odd old cuss.
So, look first into your own mirror
And you may see the bonafide furor.

For All To See

His heart they say is made of gold.
If that be true—and it may be—
They did not say "Fools Gold,"
But that's the case for all to see.

On This Plane

Hairdos, body piercing,
Face makeup, attire.
They each bespeak
Of a troublesome world.

Unfortunately, God's influence
On normalcy
Has not extended
To any of the above.

Over Seventy

The mirror on the wall
Reminds us each of yesterday—
A chance for overhaul
Lest we become a bit passe.

Waste

If one could add the time one wastes
Onto one's span of life,
I'm sure that spent awaiting flights
Would be the one with strife.

They like to say "on time," you see,
But that is just wordplay,
Because despite their act to help
You're left with more delay.

Mr. Piggy (In Flight)

To my right and skip one seat
There sits a man who's dressed quite neat
Tailored suit and paisley tie.
They fit so tight they make him sigh.

With time he drinks a little more
And to his wife he is a bore.
Now he's endowed with lots of flesh
And looks just like a pig that's fresh.

He wonders why the wife
Has tried to cut him from her life
Though never once has he seen fit
To slow intake and halt the split.

A Fact

I am sure, proportionately,
There are just as many dishonest
Non-politicians as there are
Dishonest politicians.
It is just that the perception
Is heavily weighted in the latter.

Susie, the Sow
(And her ten little pigs)

Susie, the sow,
       looked down at her ten,
And wondered how
       she had boxed herself in.
Then who walked by
       but her lover Big Ben,
And from his "eye"
       she saw another ten.

The Recycling Center

I make the biggest contributions there
Because I make such frequent trips.
And, yes, it is a worthy cause—
I'm throwing in rejection slips.

Gracious Me!

"Gracious me!" said Matilda,
"Where have you been so long?"

> *"I cannot say, Matilda dear,*
> *"But have no fear."*

"Your absence leaves much untold,
"But will you in time unfold?"

> *"Oh, yes, Matilda dear,*
> *"Quite soon it will be clear."*

"How great it will be,
"And then I will see."

> *"Yes, you will, and without doubt*
> *"You'll see I'm no roustabout."*

"Oh, how sweet of you,
"So frank and true."

> *"Now I didn't say that, Matilda dear.*
> *"You see, there're others whom I revere."*

The Aging Gent

He had no reason to suspect old age,
Except chronologically.
Not even one who called himself a sage
Could see it biologically.
But then the elements of time and space
Began to creep upon the scene.
They forced themselves and left no trace—
He was a pig, but not porcine.

Beauty

Beauty lives on
            and in various ways.
Too bad it's only inward
            in these my latter days.

Differences

The difference between us, Dear:
You see the light from the sun
And I feel only the heat.

Gambling

God would not have made woman
If He had not intended
for man to gamble.

Seventy-Nine

Yesterday I entered my 80th year,
Which means I just turned seventy-nine.
Now "old age" really offers nothng to fear
Especially when life is fine.

Hair

If all the surplus hair
From youth around so fair
Were used to help the bald
The world would be appalled.

Working Together

I used to think Old Age and I
could be friends,
But then we'd only casually met.
It was not until we were "wed"
that I knew I'd always be
within her debt.

So then we sat and had a talk
about what had been
and well might be.
I saw we both could yield a bit,
adjust our stubborn ways,
And thereby coexist
throughout the waning days.

Reminder

I like old age
        And the comfort it brings
Except I'm reminded:
        It's no longer Spring.

Replacement

Only death replaces old age,
And that's such a permanent thing.
Maybe we should give some thought
To postponing it whenever
We can.

How do we accomplish this?

One way is to avoid
Oldsters who talk only of
Their illnesses or grandchildren;
Ignore the middle-aged ones
Who talk about the weather.

How further can we accomplish this?

Try not to listen to your neighbors
Gossip about their neighbors
(One of them may be you.)
Listen to the teenagers
When they have something to say.

And believe it or not, that can happen.

Always give religious zealots
The time of day, but only
If you're wearing a watch.
And give weight to the policeman's body,
Not his word.

Age is not so much an accumulation of years
As it is a collection of burdens,
Joys and acceptances.
It is how we carry these
That really makes the difference.

Oh, Yes

I can't say that you are the one,

But if you are not, you are the twin.

Life's Unsavory Recipe

Don't try this recipe,
I'll warn you now.
It's not the usual mix:
A stir and then a bake.
It's easy to fix,
But life's not a piece of cake.

Mental Patchwork In A Relationship

I tried to patch the cracks along the way,
But the glue I used was too weak.
And if I had a chance to start anew
I'd probably use the same old glue.

MISCELLANY

A *dib, a dab, a daub*

Our Flag
(The Red, White and Blue)

She proudly waves
    all fifty stars on blue
    and thirteen stripes—
    six white and seven red.
It's steadying proof
    all love this land—
    a host to all
    including the dead.

How much longer
    before the red
    bleeds into the white,
    from senseless violence,
Or people cease their
    contempt for law and order
    and lack of compassion,
    ignoring the consequence?

Only help from above,
    a change in attitude,
    a yield to common sense,
    and a hand of kindness,
Will keep her wave intact,
    her face unblemished,
    signaling defeat
    to all who would oppress.

Quo Vadis

Man cannot wrest time from its path;
Though silent, it is too relentless,
Too permanent in movement.
Nor can the ocean's tide be heard far inland,
Despite its universal effect.
And the sun casts shadows and energies,
Offering all a chance to survive.
Yet, there still exists those who try
To destroy that which is to be,
Making no change in time,
Only a mockery of man.

The Cemetery Tree

She was once young but grew
Because she had a purpose:
To watch over those lying
Within her quiet reign.

Her trunk is mammoth, her spread
Like that of the soaring eagle.
But now she is old
And stands serene.

Many who once admired her majestic beauty
Now rest in peace within her view,
Safe from worldly cares
And troubles.

She watches over these silent souls,
Knowing that each respects her presence
As they culminate
Their earthly existence.

Yes, she will stand ever vigilant
For those who've gone before
And yet to come, until she, too,
Will join them in their journey.

Furrow

No furrow is so deep
As one that's plowed with love,
Nor soil so fresh-enriched
As that enmeshed with friends.
No growth so great within
As that which sows concern.
We are a seed, a sprout,
A plant now on our own.

No Longer The Place

I have returned for the day,
Just for the day.
I cannot again live here
For it is today not yesterday
And past memories
Are too elusive to recapture.
So today I have been here
Only today
Because yesterday has gone.

Foreign Policy

I've seen our country's open arms
To all who are our friends,
But have we not outstretched ourselves
Thus leading us to endless ends?

In Pursuit of What?

They told me life was a bowl of cherries,
    but I don't like cherries.
They offered me a bowl of prunes,
    but prunes make you run.

How about a dozen lemons?
    but I have no sugar for lemonade.
Then what will make you happy?
    Who said the sun always shines?

Ode to Momus*

Dawn left a while ago,
     yielding to the rising sun.
Beings now stir upon the Earth:
     a refuge for misplaced souls,
     well-meaning saints,
     and sinners bent on good.
Discrimination is alien to Nature
     while it mothers all,
     as each wonders why
     time means so little
     and space even less.
They fight the currents of sorrow,
     ride the shallow waves of joy
     or trek the lonely paths of indecision,
     hoping for tomorrows they do not know.

*Momus: In Greek mythology,
the god of Blame and Mockery*

Love's Collection

I sit amidst the rubbish in my life—
    alone
        alone
            alone,

A pile I did not amass today,
    or yesterday,
        but over time—
            a life's collection.

I sit alone
    alone
        alone
            too alone,

Surrounded by rubbish I cannot shed—
    alone
        alone
            alone.

Sickness

Love is the kindest illness,
      an illness with which too few
         are afflicted.

Aid

For some, sorrows are made
      to fill destinies.
With others, happiness is made
      to drown sorrows.
Both have help from self.

Ditto

Yesterday was once tomorrow,
      a tomorrow that came and went.
Tomorrow will soon be yesterday,
      and it too will be gone.
Why are they the same,
      as they come and go, come and go,
And change not their colors,
      only gray, gray, gray?

Outlook

I have not seen youth
      as the magic wand,
Nor old age
      the antidote,
But I know one's outlook is a map
      to guide to a better tomorrow.

Emotional Antonyms

Separation: that state of existence
      when mind and body cannot agree.
Togetherness: that state of existence
      when mind and body react crazily.

The Aphrodisiac

Coated with saccharin,
Lined with bitters,
Mixed with deceiving powders,
Love is not the aphrodisiac
It's touted to be.
It is an elixir for fools
Or those who aspire to be.

Suspension

I reach for tomorrows
        that may never come,
Think of yesterdays
        that I did not grasp,
And wonder if time
        will lend a hand
Or let me remain
        in this suspended state.

Dim Hope

For some, darkness comes
        not just at night,
Nor from lack of light from the sun
        or flame.
One is the path of life,
The other the road to strife.

No race is better than the next,
Nor color in the lead.
We need to drop the whole pretext,
And live by the fairness creed.

If Given

Even when opportunity
Presents the choice
For a leisurely walk through life,
Many fail to stretch their legs
Lest they stumble on
They know not what.

Quandary

I do not know why I'm here,
Nor just how long I'll stay.
I do know, though, and say with fear,
Today is not like yesteryear.

Opinion

We live in a world today so sick
I fear its patients will not survive.
Only time—if there is that—
Will prove me right or wrong.

Await

I read scripture as a child—
(My parents saw to that.)
I grew from their comments and actions.
Then I faced the world,
And loved it for a while.
But now I'm watching as it slips
Into degradation beyond description.
So, is the answer to await its demise
And suffer the consequence,
Or do we yield to Him above
And practice what He would have us do?

Attitude

Old age
Is the penalty or reward
We're given for living so long,
Depending on attitude.

The Fact

I think time has shown the human
    being for what he is:
A beast caught in a jungle
    from which he cannot escape.
Now he must fight to live from day to day
To kill, to pillage and to rape.

Must it be?

Companion

I never found a companion
More rewarding than solitude.
It gives me space and time
For enjoying wide latitude.

Democracy

We risk our lives each day
By things we do and say,
And never stop to think
It is America's way.
God bless the USA.

Gauging

Gauge not happiness by laughter,
For often it drowns the inner pain,
And leaves the listener
Without knowledge of the real you.

Time

Tomorrow is not within today's reach,
And yesterday has slipped away.
Perhaps today will fall
On outstretched arms,
And make a better way.

In Charge

Friends are essential, family, too.
You need them both, we know.
But don't forget the pets around;
It's they who run the show.

Instincts

If we replaced man's basic instincts:
>greed
>hatred
>revenge
>selfishness
>jealousy
>and fakery

And let surface—with a little help:

>love
>companionship
>selflessness
>friendship
>humaneness
>and worthy ambitions

Our world would be a paradise.

Mankind

There is no need to weep
For today's mankind.
It, too, will pass.
And then another will come on the scene,
No worse, no better,
Just different.

Horizons

Horizons reach beyond all borders,
A world phenomenon in which man has no say.
Countries accept their presence—
(They have no choice.)
The sun that rises in the East
Is sure to set in the West,
And only time measures its route.
Man, a part of the Universe,
Knows the hemispheres have two poles:
The North and the South,
And that between these all humans live,
Some peacefully, some violently.
None gain by the latter, only the former.
Were man's own horizons more far-reaching,
And earthly aims more humane,
All the world would flourish
In absolute harmonious spirit.

Metamorphosis

Birth: The process by which the warm-
blooded mammal comes upon
the universal scene in a condition
of helplessness, fragility
and innocence.

Living: That state of being
between birth and death.

Death: The end result of the combination
of *birth* and *living*,
a result so final that no
amount of reconsideration of actions
will alter the outcome.

Analysis: We are but one spoke
in the Universal wheel,
a wheel which turned before us
and will turn after we are gone.
Our contribution to Eternity
is directly proportionate
to the efforts expended
while on this plane.

It Is Within

Man walks the wooded path
in search of peace and calm.
He seldom stops to think
it lies within his palm.

Myself

I cannot tell you why I am
    the way I am today,
Nor why I was the way
    I was only yesterday.
I only know that tomorrow I will be
    a better man, a fairer man,
But still, I'll be just me.

Needs

Most needs of man unmet by man

Are all because of man:

No lesson learned, no lesson taught,

No reason, rhyme or thought.

Treasures

Treasures are found
    not just in attics, museums or buried,
They are within the each of us,
    if only we're not too hurried.

The Homeless One

Tattered and torn
(No doubt battered and worn),
She sits with bowed head lightly
    touching the dirty blanket
    draped across her tiny lap.
Her night was long; her day is now.
The frail, arthritic hands
    reach upward, slowly caress
    the matted hair, then slide down the face
    and drop onto her lap.
She steals some sleep, awakens,
    and weakly scans her world.
Then once again repose
    before the authority approaches
    and asks that she move on.
Unaware that her ragged hat
    is beneath her feet, she does,
    only to repeat her daily chore:
    Living.

Counsel

Blackberry bushes, heavily leaved,
Bow as I approach;
Offer bounteous gifts
Deep black, soft and sweet.
Yet remind me of the need
To pick with gentle care
Or else be pricked by thorns
That spring from everywhere.

And so it is with friends.

Cliffhanging

I sometimes think I was born with age,
And not because of wrinkles or brains.
It's just that yesterday has gone
And left me filled with geriatric pains.
So here I am with only now
And hope I hold onto it,
Or else I'll have to figure out
A way I can renew it.

Our Brethren

Ancient spacemen leisurely maneuver
   on their interplanetary mission,
   stare at planet Earth,
   and beam back to their sophisticated
   astronomical observatory
   interesting comparisons:

Our cars are oxen carts of Biblical days,
Our homes above-ground cavemen dwellings,
Our brains mere embryonic cells,
Our wars deadly diseases brought on
   by earthly creature's greed,
   hatred and incomplacency.

Compared to their development,
   our brethren view us as
   mere amebas, lost in space,
   waiting for the millennial tides
   to make their periodic change.

They realize that our opportunities
   are limitless,
   and know that alternating chaos and peace
   will reign until Earthbeings comply
   with the Universal Tenet:

Compassion for all mankind.

Surprises

Tolerance of perfection
Is the ultimate discretion.

    *   *   *

It's age that tries to slow man down,
But often makes him just a clown.

    *   *   *

Because my thoughts refuse
      to come with plentifulness
I sometimes think my head
      the Well of Emptiness.

Sightless Observation

Often the reason some people can't see straight
      has nothing to do with their eyes.
It's because their mind is curved
      and blocked to logic.

Dosage

They say that laughter is the best medicine,
    A cure for many ills.
If that is the case, the doctor has failed.
    I've just run out of pills.

The SoreMakers

The tales of woe as told by some
Begin from lack of self-esteem,
A quirk within the craniumn
That plays into the dirty scheme.
If each afflicted with this dread
Began to see himself the bore,
Perhaps he'd try to leave unsaid
The things that make us all so sore.

From Obscurity To Oblivion

We enter this chasm
    of human turmoil
    with nothing to share
    even our body's bare.

Oh, there's flesh
    and certainly breath,
    which we are granted
    from God who planted.

But once our role is played
    we must let it be,
    as we pass over the horizon
    into oblivion.

Some Of The Past

Some remembrances
    of the past
Are faded
    bouquets
Yet unremoved
    from the vase of life.

The Stairs

I walked
      on down
            the stairs
                  of time
            and saw
      the last
    short rung
was near.
      'Twas then
        I knew
            the word
                  "sublime"
            had failed
    again
to reappear.

AGING IS:

...Nature's way of passing time.

...God putting the finishing touches
   on His greatest masterpiece.

...the reservoir of life.

...our Creator's fulfillment of His trust
   in man.

...life lightly knocking to remind us
   to live each day with a plan for
   tomorrow that includes respecting
   our fellowman.

...the Master's way of giving depth,
   character and inner beauty
   to His most precious work.

...a prop to enhance living and
   further learning.

Opportunity

The good in people will come out
If given half a chance.
So let there be no doubt
It's love paid in advance.

The Final

Colorful sprays, tall vases
Filled with Nature's finest art,
Wreaths of soft beauty
Surround the casket and spread
Among its solemn space.

Family, friends, even some curious,
Sit or stand,
Listening to the good man
Drop words of praise
As easily as breathing.

Tears and sobs roam the room
As handkerchiefs meet bowed heads.

It is over now,
A life given to many.
Those left return to their homes,
Live in temporary sorrow—
Some longer than others.

Tomorrow the sun will rise.
Life will go on,
Until another is called,
Signaling the need to gather again
Among sprays, vases, wreaths and words.

My Trips

Of all the trips to here and yon
The ones I like the best
Are those that leave me very fond
Of things at my behest.

They range from flight to food
To sights I choose to see,
But most of all the ones that suit
Are those of fantasy.

Passing

If youngsters learned their lessons
There'd be no failing grades.
The solution is an easy one:
More digging with mental spades.

The Porch

Sitting on the porch of old age
The view can be quite vast;
But only if at that late stage
We dwell not on the past.

The Doctor's Receptionist

Patients arrive, stand at the window behind
    the icy glass, and wait for the receptionist to
    acknowledge them.
She is oblivious except to her world of self-concern.
    (They are just another Medicare number, a
    Blue Shield policy, a "private awaiting the
Sergeant's orders.")

Compassion is no friend of hers;
    only the weekly check.

Her hair is blonde today. Yesterday it rode the
    sparks of electricity to unbelievable heights,
    and failed to lie back down.
But she'll be all right if time allows,
    for God knew what he was doing
    when he made people like her,
    many of them.

He had to have an example to teach the
    rest of us how not to be.

The Others

The trouble with people:
    they're not themselves.
But if they were
    we could be ourselves.

Words

Words, an essential part of life,
Used to free or bind,
Bring joy or sadness,
Depending on what's behind.
But none are as needed
As words that show we're kind.

Utopian Dream

When rich begin to rule it's called plutocracy,
And if it is the poor, they say ptochocracy.
But let us stop and think, if each exchanged his rank
They both might be replaced by true democracy.

Unwarranted Treatment

I looked across the field
At crops I had not sowed.
'Twas then I saw the yield
Of things I was not owed.

Crossroads

(National Court Reporters Association)

We are professionals among professionals,
The silent captors of the word;
Essential cogs in the wheels of justice
For America's litigious herd.

We are professionals among professionals,
And strive to stay that way,
But embrace technology as "a helping hand."
We record the world today.

A Guidepost

Given time
Everyone breathes the essence of life—
Some more deeply than others.
But it is the vision we clasp
That motivates our being
And steadies the course
We finally take.

Why?

I can't believe the minds of some,
Nor why they have such hate.
But could it be their cranium
Was bent that way by fate?

A Deed in Defeat

As generous as it may seem
      to feed the many poor,
It leads our worldly team
      to many, many more.

Life's Facade

Lace is the trimming
      we stitch outside
To compensate for the patch
      we failed to sew inside.

Misjudging

No head can tell the heart just what to do
      when the heart is drowned in joy,
Because it beats without a clue
      and plays a tricky ploy.

Room 620
(Dallas Hotel)

Outside the window are the lights
That glitter, beam and shine.
They represent both man and sites,
And most by planned design.

But here within these papered walls
I sit upon a chair
And wonder why there are no calls,
Instead, so much despair.

More Care

We know that some were born to help
And others born that need just that.
But haven't those who only whelp
Considered, yes, the rightful fact
That each should first begin to run
Affairs that stem from being dense,
And stop this propogation "fun" —
Just use a lot more common sense.

The Way

The way
We look at life
Can have a great effect
On all the happiness we each
Collect.

The Troubled World

The soil beneath our shaky feet
Provides a base to build.
It guarantees a place to meet
And common ground for yield.

The rest is up to man alone
To cure the numerous ills,
And work to have us each atone
For all our senseless kills.

Mortal

Nothing wreaks more heavily,
    though sometimes silently,
Than man's attempt
    at being different.
And through it all
    he is the same:

A fallible mortal being.

Lonesome At The Airport

Amid the crowd of human heads I sit,
   silently watching them go by.
Now and then one passes with credentials
   of interest,
But most of mankind (to me at least) are
   reproductions, not originals,
And as such offer little
   of lasting value.

Oh, they breathe our air, expel, of course.
They hide themselves with props—
   some with many, some with few.

"Are you Woody Brown?" asks a youthful passerby.
"No," I say, almost abrupt in manner.
"I'm sorry," he says. "I guess everybody
   has to look like somebody."
"You're right," I said. He left.

A child of three walks by. What is his future?
   Neither he nor the child were originals.

But what does one do if he lives in the world?
He must, of course, accept the rest.
And it might not be a bad idea
   if he looks in the mirror.
For then, even he might see a reproduction.

And if that so be, why expect more of the rest?
More, that is, than he himself offers.
Think about it and then act. It is up to you,
For lonesomeness does not have to be.

Friends

True friends
Are the best therapists.
They listen
Without regard to time,
Comment without fear of repercussion,
Understand and tolerate,
Absorb a bit of you,
And become a part thereof.
In so doing
They offer that needed help
That makes you the special person
You want to be.

Gutter Inlet

Such reprobates I've never seen,
Nor do I care to mingle with.
But none of them are truly mean,
Just wading in the murky frith.

122

Happiness

Happiness, real happiness,
Is a state of being
Where one's inner self
Is in harmony with the outer self.

When the two are in concert
It's beautiful indeed.
The mind flows freely,
And the body acts with zest.

There exists a radiance,
Albeit of varying degrees,
That defies description,
For it is intangible, almost subliminal.

Happiness, real happiness,
Is rare,
But it is a goal
To which more should aspire.

For then, and only then,
Will each of us
Reach our full
Potential.

JUSTICE

Were that it was,
As the word implies,
But we all know—
At least most of us—

That Justice for one
Can be punishment for another,
Fairness to some
Inequity to others.

So what does one do
In this world of ours,
When those offended—
Be it to what degree—

Are victims
Of those who seek
To gain by motives
So foreign to truth?

The answer lies not always
In the courts of our land—
Though we've all seen examples
Where it works both ways.

The solution probably remains
Illusive and pale,
At least for the time being,
And maybe longer.

But given opportunity,
Compensation will come into play;
And then, for us, and others, too,
Justice will offer its hand.

And when it does,
It's then we'll become aware
That there is some fairness
For those who wait and share.

The Wealthy at The Inn

I sit, I see, I hear,
      and am convinced:
Age is no gauge of wisdom,
Laughter no sign of joy,
Nor money a respecter of beauty.
For in their faces are
      crevices of ugliness,
      lines of wanton despair,
      and layers of aged hurt.
They came seeking something
      (God knows what),
      and dot the place
      like blackbirds
      criss-crossing a field,
Before returning once again
      to where they sleep and wake,
      to begin another day of the same.
These are the wealthy at The Inn.

Entwined

Who can figure out the human race
When it's so entwined with mental lace?

Hate

Hate rules from without
Affecting only those
Who are not ruled from within.

Life - A Three-Act Play

Act I   -   The Problem?

> Empty room
> Damaged heart
> Punctured by time
> Circumstances
> Infatuation
> And false hope

Act II   -   The Future?

> Beyond the walls
> Maybe tomorrow
> Will hold the answer
> Relief or grief
> Or both, as He wills

Act III   -   The Solution?

> Zigzagging along
> Never letting us know
> What's next
> But we walk
> The roads
> The trails
> The paths
> We fail
> We start anew
> For better or for worse
>
> Or both

Clover

People are clover in the field—
Many with three leaves,
Few with four.
Those are the ones
We treasure most.

A Woman's Dream

The man or beast I'd like to know
Is not the one who knows it all.
He is instead the one aglow
Who can learn to love a shopping mall.

Hopeful

I stand on the ledge of time,
        Knowing the fall is steep.
But clothed in years of love and joy
        May others now not weep.

Hollow Legacy

Many of our youth will try life
Flaunt their senseless foolishness
Caring not the consequence
For such inane behavior.
They inhale rebellion
Savor its essence
Exhale destruction
Without remorse.

They are a youth born not to bring forth
The best in man, rather,
A youth led astray
And mostly by inner self.
They forget yesterdays
Cast aside tomorrows
Then touch a slice of death
And soak in its remains.

They are a youth destined
To leave nothing worthwhile
For the generations that follow
If such comes to be.
And they do all this
In the name of, "I am Me, I've got to be,"
Out of selfish thought
For their moment in time.

Too late will they learn
That only time and age
Will be their benefactor
Whether for good or evil.

Time Marches On

Birth, health and growth
    bring us to maturity,
Depending on outlook and practice
    throughout the years.
We make of life
    what we choose.
Decline then rears its devilish head
    and judges well our past.
One last time
    we reach out,
Or shrink into smaller beings,
    resting on our laurels,
Before returning whence we came,
    leaving others who will follow.

An Opinion

One's time upon this earth
Is judged by years of life.
Better by far since birth
To cancel those of strife.

Without Enrichment

If all of me were meant for you,
And none were left for me,
I'd have to say we never grew
Beyond our selfish plea.

As such, we'd try to satiate
The hearty thirst for each
And in effect emasculate
The inner goal we'd reach.

"A Friend"

Words, lines, paragraphs,
Chapters, books, and even volumes,
Have been written
On the definition of "a friend."

But I think it all unnecessary,
Because it is not the written word
That truly expresses it so well;
It is the feeling, the actions,

The inner self,
That tells you how it really is.
And that constitutes the bounds
For the definition of "a friend."

A Sea

A sea of people
Ride this L-1011,
All headed to
Different shores.

Interesting it would be
To know their destinations,
And reasons therefor.
Indeed it would.

But such is not
My province,
Nor theirs to know of mine;
And thus it will be.

Humanity being what it is,
Mobile, and fleetingly so,
We must each resign ourselves
To be just another within the sea.

In Spite Of

Each year I see your face,
　　　　Those lines I can't erase.
It matters not, my dear,
　　　　You cloud all doubt and fear.

His Brother's Funeral

His brother Ted is home today,
Back from a trip he did not plan.
He turned his back and walked away
To seek, he thought, a better clan.

He used his strength and wandering mind
To try and boost some sad egos.
He moved ahead as one who's blind
Because he loved the highs and lows.

The toll it took on one so young,
Who could have gone so far in life,
Has left his praise and good unsung—
The victim now of drugs and strife.

In School Today

The things they learn in school today
Are not the things to show the way.
They learn to lie and cheat in stealth
To get the things that we call "wealth."

What they really need are:

The values taught in olden times
By those now in their golden primes:
To read, to write, to understand,
That man needs man if he's to stand.

Randy

The victim of a
Thoughtless driver
Bent on cruelty,
Cold macadam now offers
The only final resting place
For this small creature
Who lost the race
To cross the road.

Little by little
His body will be interred,
Crushed into rough surfaces,
As unsuspecting motorists,
Sun, and rain take their turn.
Another day, another loss,
Another of man's friends:
Randy, the squirrel.

An Honest Opportunity

Our young reward the old
In ways as yet untold.
They meld the truth and fact
And often then react.

So, though it seems at times
They stop just short of crimes,
If we just think it through,
It's to themselves they're true.

The old, too slow to cede,
Beneath their ancient creed,
Could learn from this new breed,
And cause us to be freed.

TORO DE LIDIA
(The Bull of Combat)

Man lives by his bravery;
    the bull must die from it.

So it is his desire to charge
    that brings about his demise
    among a roaring crowd.

And when aroused,
    the muscles of his neck
    swell thick.

It is not the color of the cape
    that is the prime agitator,
    but the movement that aggravates.

And should the matador
    lose control
    and fail to coolly meet the charge,

The thrust of horns
    by the enraged beast
    can do much harm.

But the matador demonstrates his art
    as he astutely defends himself in drama
    drawn from danger, bloodshed and death.

And he must execute his moves with
    certain techniques: veronicas, farols,
    gaoneras and reboleras.

And once he has performed
    so masterfully,
    and ready for the kill,

The crowd is on edge
    as it awaits
    the final plunge.

If successful,
    in bravery and artistry,
    they will applaud.

And even wave the handkerchief,
    demanding an ear be awarded
    the matador.

It is then, among roaring admirers,
    he accepts, and proudly circles the ring,
    once again victorious—vainglorious.